CUSTOMS · COSTUMES AND CULTURES

JEWELRY

by
Kevin K. Casey

Rourke Publications, Inc.
Vero Beach, Florida 32964

ACKNOWLEDGEMENTS

I would like to thank Jerry Craven for many of the photographs and for assistance in the research for this book. I also thank Photophile of San Diego, California, and Picture Library Associates of Guadalupe, California.

PHOTO CREDITS

© Photophile, L.L.T. Rhodes: page 4; © Photophile, Robert W. Ginn: page 5; © Kevin K. Casey: pages 6 and 21; © Jerry Craven: pages 7, 8, 9, 10, 11, 13, 14, 15, 16, 19, 22, 23, 24, 25, 26, 27, 28 and 29; © Photophile, Glasheen Graphics: page 30.

Library of Congress Cataloging-in-Publication Data

Casey, Kevin K., 1967-
    Jewelry / by Kevin K. Casey.
       p. cm. — (Customs, costumes, and cultures)
    Includes index.
    Summary: Examines the uses of jewelry in different cultures around the world.
    ISBN 0-86625-597-4
    1. Jewelry—Juvenile literature. [1. Jewelry.] I. Title. II. Series.
GT2250.C37   1996
391'.7—dc20   96-26593
                                                   CIP
                                                      AC

TABLE OF CONTENTS

CHAPTER 1
The Many Reasons for Jewelry

People wear jewelry for many different reasons. Sometimes they want to show how wealthy they are. Other times people wear jewelry for religious reasons. Many people believe that some kinds of jewelry can protect them from bad luck. In western countries like the United States, some adults wear wedding rings to show that they are married.

People all over the world wear jewelry.

4

This young Native American at a Cherokee Nation gathering wears a traditional costume with beaded jewelry.

Another reason that people wear jewelry is to celebrate their heritage, or past. Many cultures around the world are famous for the kinds of jewelry that they make and wear.

People all over the world give friends and relatives jewelry as gifts. Expensive watches decorated with gold and jewels are popular. Not all jewelry has a use, or purpose, like a wrist watch. Sometimes people wear jewelry just because they think it is beautiful and that it makes them look better.

One common occasion for giving gifts of jewelry is a person's birthday. Each month of the year has its own gem, called a birthstone. People give their friends and relatives jewelry made with their birthstones.

Understanding what people wear as jewelry, and why people wear it, is one way of learning about other cultures.

CHAPTER 2
Bones and Teeth

Some of the first materials people used for jewelry were parts from animals. Ancient people all over the world made headdresses from bird feathers. Wearing feathers might have shown that a man was the chief of a tribe. Tribes might also give feathers to warriors for bravery in battle.

Many ancient people made jewelry from the horns of large animals like buffalos and rams. Tribe members wore headdresses and other jewelry made from horns to show their rank, or importance, within the tribe.

This man in Mexico polishes amber and makes it into rings and pendants.

Jewelry carved into the shape of animal bones, teeth, and claws is still popular today.

Some people made jewelry from teeth. Many of the native tribes of Australia made necklaces from crocodile and kangaroo teeth. Both men and women wore these necklaces. In Australia, **archaeologists** (ar kee AH luh jists) have found necklaces made from teeth that are over 6,000 years old.

Another early source of materials for jewelry came from trees. **Amber** (AM ber) is sap from pine trees that died millions of years ago. Amber is not soft like the sap in living trees. It is hard because it has **fossilized** (FAH suh liizd). Pieces of beautiful yellow and gold amber sometimes wash up onto the beaches in Northern Europe. Jewelers have made these pieces into jewelry for thousands of years. In France and Spain, archaeologists have found amber jewelry in 17,000-year-old graves.

CHAPTER 3
Gold

People have valued gold for a long time. The ancient Egyptians made jewelry from gold over 5,000 years ago. The archaeologist who discovered the ancient city of Troy, on the western coast of what is now Turkey, found gold jewelry over 4,500 years old.

Gold has remained popular all through history. Today people use gold more than any other metal to make jewelry. People all over the world wear gold jewelry: gold rings, watches, necklaces, and earrings. Sometimes jewelers put gems like diamonds or rubies into gold rings.

Some cultures use gold jewelry in religious ceremonies.

A wall in the Imperial Palace in Bangkok, Thailand, is decorated with gold painted statues and jewels.

One reason that gold is so popular is because it is easy for jewelers to work with. Pure gold is soft and easy to bend. When they combine gold with other metals it becomes harder and stronger.

People in different parts of the world have different customs about wearing gold jewelry. Many Chinese believe that wearing gold can bring good luck. Some Chinese do not like gold mixed with other metals. They believe that pure gold brings more luck than gold mixed with other metals.

CHAPTER 4
The Lucky Gemstone

Many Chinese believe that jade is a lucky gemstone. Some believe jade jewelry can bring the wearer good luck, especially when it is combined with gold. Chinese men in Southeast Asia often wear a gold ring with a jade stone in the center. The gold part of the ring also has carvings of a dragon and a **phoenix** (FEE niks), a legendary bird. The Chinese men who wear these rings believe that both the dragon and the phoenix are lucky beasts.

Jade is popular in other parts of Asia, too. In Thailand, many people wear jade on a gold chain necklace. The jade is carved into a circle. The circle stands for eternity, or forever, and sometimes eternal love.

Many people in Thailand believe that wearing jade jewelry will bring them good luck.

Jade is the national gemstone of Costa Rica. These pieces were carved by Native Americans.

The Maori of New Zealand also make jewelry from jade. Jade necklaces, broaches, and earrings are important to Maori families. The Maori call jade "green stone." In the past, Maori warriors used weapons made from jade.

Maoris also wore pendants called *hei-tiki* (hey TEE kee). Hei means "hanging," and tiki means "person." One legend says that the hei-tiki pendants stand for the first person created by Tane, a Maori god. Today many Maori women wear hei-tiki pendants that have been passed down in their families for many years.

11

CHAPTER 5
The Unlucky Gemstone

About 100 years ago, many people in Europe and the United States read a novel about a gem that brought its owners bad luck. The gem was a piece of blue moonstone. While the novel was popular, many people in the United States and Europe stopped buying jewelry made from moonstone. However, people in other parts of the world still bought moonstone. Later in the 20th century, people in Europe and the United States no longer believed that moonstone was unlucky, but it was too late. The world's supply of blue moonstone was gone.

Moonstone is popular today, but it is hard to find. For many years the world's best blue moonstone came from the island of Sri Lanka, off the coast of India. In 1987, miners in Sri Lanka took the last of the moonstone from the ground.

Part of the reason so many people want moonstone is that it is one of the birthstones for the month of June. In the past, people in most of the world bought moonstone when they could not find or afford pearls, the other birthstone for June. However in Germany and Switzerland, people bought pearls when they could not get moonstone. Moonstone was more popular than pearls because moonstones can be found in the Swiss Alps. Today, moonstone is still popular, but because moonstone is so hard to find, most people born in June wear pearls.

The world's supply of blue moonstone from Sri Lanka is gone, but there are many other beautiful gemstones that are used in jewelry.

CHAPTER 6
Turquoise and Silver

When the first Spanish explorers traveled through what is now the southwestern part of the United States, they noticed that the Native Americans wore a greenish-blue stone called turquoise. The Native Americans made jewelry from turquoise and had many mines. There were at least 200 ancient turquoise mines. Some historians believe that Native Americans have been making turquoise jewelry for over 2,000 years.

Some Native American tribes, like the Navajo, believe that turquoise can bring good luck. Hunters often put a piece of turquoise on their rifles to help them shoot straight. Some Native Americans believe that putting turquoise in their hair will protect them from lightning and snake bites.

Native American jewelry is popular all over the world. This salesman from India sells jewelry made by Native Americans in the southwestern United States.

Many Native American tribes also made jewelry from silver. When combined with turquoise, silver was especially valuable to the Native Americans. Sometimes Native American jewelers strung pieces of turquoise into necklaces. They also set pieces of turquoise into jewelry like bracelets or silver pins in the shape of animals.

Native American silver and turquoise jewelry is still popular today. Many people in the United States and other places in the world admire it. Some tribes like the Navajo, Hopi, and Zuni have become famous for their beautiful silver and turquoise jewelry.

Native American jewelers still make many different kinds of turquoise jewelry.

CHAPTER 7
Green, Red, and Blue

People have prized emeralds for a long time. The ancient Egyptians mined this green gem over 3,000 years ago. To the ancient Greeks, the emerald was a symbol of Aphrodite, the goddess of love. Many people in the ancient world believed staring at an emerald was good for a person's eyes.

Today most emeralds come from Colombia, in South America. Emeralds are one of the rarest and most valuable gems. Though not as hard as diamonds, rubies, or sapphires, emeralds are hard gems. They are popular stones for all kinds of jewelry.

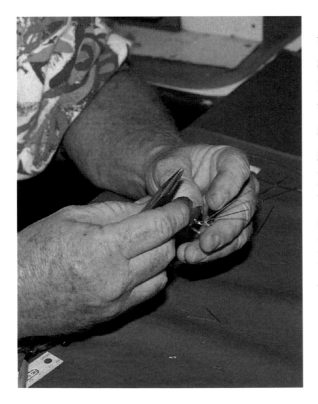

People have also treasured rubies and sapphires. Long ago, many people believed that rubies and sapphires, like other gems, had magical powers. They believed that wearing rubies or sapphires could protect a person from all sorts of things, including bad weather.

This jeweler is mounting a ruby in a gold ring.

Rubies and sapphires come from the same gemstone, called **corundum** (kuh RUN dum). Red corundum is ruby, and blue corundum is sapphire. Today the most valuable rubies are a deep red color. They are called "pigeon's blood" rubies. These rubies come from Burma in Southeast Asia.

Many of the world's best sapphires come from the city of Ratnapura in Sri Lanka. Ratnapura means "city of gems." Some large sapphires come from high in the Himalaya Mountains in India.

BIRTHSTONES

Month	Stone
January	Garnet
February	Amethyst
March	Bloodstone or Aquamarine
April	Diamond
May	Emerald
June	Pearl or Moonstone
July	Ruby
August	Sadonyx or Peridot
September	Sapphire
October	Opal or Tourmaline
November	Topaz
December	Turquoise

CHAPTER 8
The Hardest Gemstone

Most historians believe that India was the first place where people mined diamonds and made them into jewelry. Long ago, some Indian diamonds were taken to the Roman Empire. The Romans believed that the diamonds had magical powers. Arabian merchants took diamonds to China. There, craftsmen used the hard stone to carve jade.

As Indian diamonds spread throughout the world, so did many of the Indians' beliefs about diamonds. Hundreds of years ago, many people believed that swallowing a diamond could bring energy and good health. Many Europeans also believed that diamonds could keep away evil spirits and nightmares.

Diamonds are the hardest gemstone. They are made of pure carbon, formed deep inside the Earth under great pressure and high temperatures. Diamonds are so hard that they can cut glass and many other materials.

In 1867, a boy stumbled onto one of the best places in the world to find diamonds. Erasmus Jacobs was playing on the bank of a river near his family's farm in South Africa. While he was playing, he saw many shiny pebbles. Erasmus took the best ones home. One day a neighbor was admiring one of Erasmus' pebbles, so Erasmus gave it to him. The neighbor sold the pebble to a lion hunter, who recognized it as a diamond. Soon everyone heard about the discovery of diamonds in South Africa. Today South Africa is a major producer of diamonds.

Jewelers cut diamonds and other gems into many different shapes and sizes.

BLACK DIAMONDS

Not all diamonds are clear as glass. Some diamonds are yellow, green, blue, pink, red, or black. Jewelers and other people in the industry use black diamonds called *carbonado* that can cut almost anything—including other diamonds.

CHAPTER 9
Jewels from the Sea

Pearls are as popular today as they have ever been. Some historians believe that people have admired pearls for over 5,500 years. Many legends tell stories about how pearls were created. One Oriental legend says that pearls are made by moonbeams striking the sea. A Christian legend says that the tears of Adam and Eve turned into pearls.

Some oysters in the ocean, and some clams in rivers and lakes, make pearls. Oysters and clams belong to a family of shellfish called mollusks. When a grain of sand or a piece of shell gets caught inside an oyster, the oyster covers the grain with a material called mother-of-pearl. The oyster does this to protect itself from the sharp grain or piece of shell. After a few years, the oyster covers the grain with so much mother-of-pearl that it is large enough to be a pearl.

Today pearls come from several different places. Valuable black pearls come from Tahiti. In Japan, people put pieces of shells inside oysters to help them make pearls. These pearls are called "cultured" pearls. Sometimes people in the United States find pearls in the clams that come from rivers.

In some places, divers still collect pearls. Many of these divers do not use any modern tools to help them breathe underwater. Some of these divers can hold their breath for over two minutes. In Japan, young women dive for shells. These young women are called "Daughters of the Sea."

Pearls are as popular today as they were thousands of years ago.

CHAPTER 10
Shells and Coral

The remains of dead sea creatures provided the material for some of the earliest jewelry. Archaeologists have discovered that jewelry made from shells or coral is one of the oldest kinds of jewelry. All ancient civilizations, including the Egyptians and the Mesopotamians, made jewelry from coral and shells. Both shells and coral are still popular today.

Until a few hundred years ago, scientists believed that coral was a kind of sea plant. Today scientists know that coral and coral reefs are the remains of tiny sea creatures called polyps. After pieces of coral are taken from the ocean, jewelers cut, polish, and sometimes carve the pieces into jewelry. The most popular kind of coral for jewelry is a red coral called **corallium** (KOR a lee um).

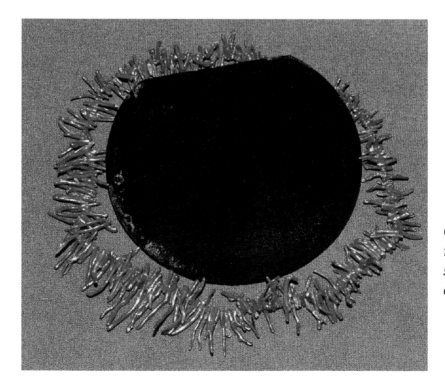

Coral is the remains of tiny sea creatures called polyps.

The red coral used in jewelry is called corallium.

People all over the world like to wear jewelry made from shells—even people who live far from the sea. In the past, Native Americans of the southwestern United States traded turquoise to other Native Americans for shells. Africans often put shells on traditional masks.

Abalone shells from the California coast are some of the most colorful shells used in jewelry. Jewelers put pieces of abalone shells under clear quartz or glass to make sparkling, colorful jewelry.

CHAPTER 11
Flowers and Tattoos

People in Hawaii often wear necklaces made from flowers. These necklaces are called **leis** (LAYS). In the past, leis were made from the feathers of island birds. Today, Hawaiians make leis from many different island flowers. It takes between 35 and 75 flowers to make one lei. Some Hawaiians give leis to guests when they arrive and when they leave.

Jewelry made from metal, stones, or plants is not the only way some cultures decorate their bodies. Tattoos are another way of decorating a person's skin. People make tattoos by putting ink into their skin. Tattoos are permanent decorations. They will not wash or wear off.

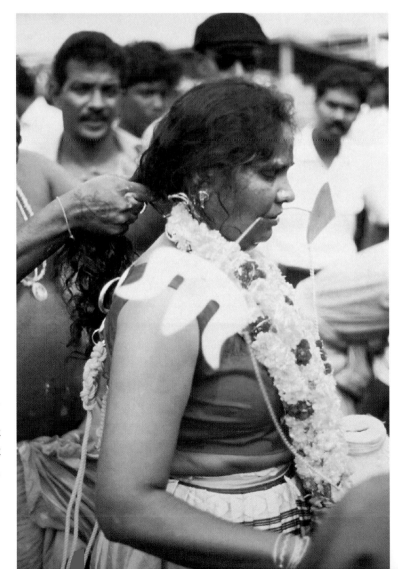

This Hindu woman in Malaysia prepares for a religious ceremony.

A man of the Iban tribe in Borneo has earned his tatoos by capturing the heads of enemy tribesmen.

In western countries like the United States, people wear tattoos as decorations. People in other areas of the world wear tattoos for more serious reasons. In Southeast Asia, there are tribes that wear special tattoos. In some of these tribes, men get tattoos as a reward for being head hunters. Warriors from one tribe sometimes take the heads of warriors from enemy tribes. When a warrior brings home an enemy's head, he gets a tattoo and is respected by everyone in his tribe.

CHAPTER 12
Jewelry and Religion

Many cultures use jewelry for religious reasons. Sometimes people wear jewelry to show others which religion they follow. Other times people wear jewelry during religious rituals.

Roman Catholicism is a common religion in Europe, North America, and South America. Many Roman Catholics wear jewelry that stands for their religion. Some Roman Catholics wear necklaces with a cross-shaped pendant. Rosary beads are another common piece of Roman Catholic jewelry. Many Roman Catholics hold rosary beads while praying.

A man shows his belief in the Hindu gods by attaching limes to his chest with fish hooks.

This child wears a traditional flower necklace used in Hindu religious rituals.

Jewelry is important in religious practices in Asia. At the Batu Caves Temple in Malaysia, Hindus show their faith by wearing several types of jewelry. One type of jewelry is made from fruit like lemons or limes. The Hindus attach the fruit to their bodies with fish hooks. Another kind of jewelry is a necklace made from flowers.

Many Islamic people wear gold jewelry, but not into a mosque, or place of worship. Some Islamic people believe that it is acceptable to wear gold jewelry into a mosque as long as the jewelry is only one-third pure gold. Gold that is only one-third pure looks more like copper than gold.

Hindu men in Katmandu, Nepal, make flower necklaces and give them to people who have brought relatives to a nearby hospital.

CHAPTER 13
Modern American Jewelry

These three university students wear special medals to show that they are members of an honor society.

Jewelry is an important part of modern American culture. Some people wear jewelry because they like the way it looks. Other people wear jewelry to show something they have done or something they believe in.

One of the most common reasons for wearing jewelry is marriage. When two people decide to get married, the man often gives the woman an engagement ring. One kind of engagement ring is gold with a single diamond, called a diamond solitaire. During marriage ceremonies the bride and groom exchange wedding rings. The most popular kind of wedding rings are made of gold.

Many Americans wear jewelry that shows where they went to school. When young Americans graduate from high school, they often buy gold rings that show the name of their school and the year they graduated. These rings are called class rings. In addition to colored gemstones, many class rings have symbols like footballs or tennis rackets that show the sports the student played while in high school.

Some people get jewelry as a reward for winning a contest or for hard work. When athletes win races or tournaments, they sometimes get medals that they wear around their necks. After people have worked at a job for a long time, they retire. Many American companies give retiring employees gold watches to thank them for years of hard work.

Most married Americans wear rings to show that they are married.

CHAPTER 14
Jewelry Today

Since the first people saw shiny gems and thought they were beautiful, jewelry has been a part of life all over the world. Jewelry is important to people for many reasons including religion and heritage.

Many people admire jewelry for its beauty. Just as some people like to wear beautiful clothes, people enjoy wearing jewelry because they believe it makes them more beautiful. As long as people admire flowers, art, and all beautiful things, people will appreciate jewelry.

In many parts of the world, jewelry is a part of traditional costumes.

GLOSSARY

amber (AM bur) – yellow fossilized tree sap.

archeologist (ar kee AH luh jist)– a scientist who learns about people by studying the things they made and used.

corallium (KOR a lee um) – red coral used in making jewelry.

corundum (kuh RUN dum) – the mineral that rubies and sapphires come from.

fossilized (FAH suh liizd) – plant or animal remains that have changed into minerals over millions of years.

hei-tiki (hey TEE kee) – a jade pendant worn by the Maori of New Zealand.

lei (LAY) – a Hawaiian flower necklace.

phoenix (FEE niks) – a mythological, or legendary, bird that could live for over 500 years, then burn to death and live again.

INDEX